THE POWER
TO CHANGE
ANYTHING

GREGORY DICKOW

The Power to Change Anything
©2003 by Gregory Dickow Ministries.

All rights reserved.

Unless otherwise noted, all Scripture quotations in this
volume are from the *King James Version* of the Bible.

Printed in the United States of America

For information, please write
Gregory Dickow Ministries,
P.O. Box 7000
Chicago, IL 60680

or visit us online at www.changinglives.org.

TABLE OF CONTENTS

I'VE GOT THE POWER

Introduction

Recently, I found myself on an airplane watching a movie that I had initially rejected and dismissed as silly and irreverent.

(But then I realized, that my watching it might help me relate better to my children, my audience and society in general. *Yeah, right!)*

In the movie *Bruce Almighty*, Jim Carrey depicts a cynical, frustrated reporter searching for help, crying out to God to intervene in his life and prove He exists. When God (played by Morgan Freeman), shows up in Carrey's life, He bestows His power on him and gives him the ability to use that power in any way he sees fit. Endued with supernatural ability, we find Carrey cheerfully and somewhat maniacally, miming the words to a song, "I've got the power…"

After using this power to try to change everything around him—in order to make himself happy, he ultimately comes to the conclusion that the only way to be happy is to change himself.

That power was available to him the whole time. And that power is available to you and I right now!

In the Marine Corps there is a saying, "Unhappiness doesn't come from the way things are, *but rather from a difference in the way things are and the way we believe they should be.*"

Perhaps your life is not the way you believe it should be—this causes unhappiness.

Perhaps your job or your finances are not the way you believe they should be. Maybe it's your marriage, your body, or any of the circumstances you are facing.

If things are not the way you believe they should be, DON'T PANIC. You've got the power—to change them!

Unfortunately, we live in a society that loves the results of change but hates the process.

If I held up a Duncan Hines cake box, and you loved chocolate cake, you would admire the picture on the front of the box. You would desire the picture on the front of the box. But you wouldn't enjoy it unless you followed the instructions on the back of the box!

There are countless Christians who have been discouraged because they have been enamored by the great preaching that draws beautiful pictures of the Christian life, but often neglects to show the process or give the instructions.

This process is the simple, yet necessary step to having what we see on the front of the box. And I want to show you that process to change!

Everyone has something in their life they would like to see changed. Whether it is in a relationship, their body, in their finances or in their heart—everyone wants a change. But often we don't know how to change. That is what this book is about: how to change anything in your life.

Paul said in 2 Timothy 1:7, "God has not given us the spirit of fear, but a spirit of power." What kind of power? The power to change!

Let's begin by looking at a miracle of change in John 5:2-4 and see how to make it work in our lives today:

"Now there was in Jerusalem by the sheep market a pool which is called in the Hebrew tongue, Bethesda, having five porches. In these lay a great multitude of impotent people, blind, halt, withered, waiting for the moving of the water. For an angel went down at a certain season into the pool, and troubled the water; whosoever then first after the troubling of the water stepped in was made whole of whatsoever disease he had."

Often our miracle of change is in the midst of troubled waters, and human nature does not like that.

The Spirit of God through an angel would literally stir up these waters—and then the first person that would get into the troubled water would get healed.

And why is that? Because it takes faith to get into the midst of troubled water. The person who steps into the pool is living by faith.

There are troubled times that we all live in. The Bible says, "Don't be discouraged, you will have trouble in this life" (John 16:33). But we can step into the whirlwind, knowing that it doesn't matter what kind of trouble we're facing. We can say, "God is on my side! God is for me, not against me! God is with me and therefore no matter what waters are stirring, no matter what trouble is stirring, I will be changed in the midst of this situation!"

Sometimes we look for the calmest atmosphere so that we can find peace. But Jesus found peace in the midst of a storm! And if Jesus traveled in the midst of a storm, should we expect that we will never have to face a storm?

Change is one of those storms that we need to step into. Change brings turbulence, doesn't it? Sometimes change brings trouble.

Sometimes change brings unrest. Sometimes change brings some feelings that we don't always want to identify with. But if we're going to better our future, we've got to disturb the present sometimes.

In other words, your goal in life should not be peace. Your goal in life should be what God says—and in the end, ultimately, you will obtain that peace. But on the way, you will go through some storms. Some of those storms involve change.

We can't get away from it. It's ridiculous for Christians to think that they should try to live their lives to avoid trials. Don't live your life to avoid trials. Live your life! One day soon we're going to go home to be with Jesus. But in the meantime, God wants us to live a victorious life on this earth. He's called us to be "more than conquerors" (Romans 8:37). We all get in trials. We all get in trouble at times. We all face tough situations. But it's what we do about it that determines how great of a life we live.

Proverbs 3:13 says, "Happy is the man that finds wisdom and the man who gets understanding; for her profit is better than silver and gold; and all the things you desire cannot compare to getting understanding."

If I can get you to understand what I'm talking about, you will have something greater than riches—*you will have power!*

Every negative feeling, every fear, every form of depression comes from a sense of powerlessness. When we feel powerless to change our situation, we get frustrated, discouraged and a downward spiral begins to characterize our life.

Empowerment vs. Entitlement. The idea of *empowerment*, rather than *entitlement* is an idea whose time has come. Many people feel they are "entitled" to certain rights and privileges, but the fact is, we are not entitled to anything. We are "empowered" to obtain the rights and privileges that are available to us.

Where does this empowerment come from? From Jesus Christ, of course—the most powerful man in the universe!

Before we go on, let's look at some things we *don't* have the power to change. And when we stop trying to change those things, we will eliminate a major portion of frustration from our lives.

What We Can't Change. There are some things that we can't change and we shouldn't waste time trying to.

- Other people–(particularly, our husband, our wife, and our mother-in-law!)

- Our color—(you're beautiful!)

- Our sex—(although some have tried)

- God's will—(He is faithful!)

As we go through this passage in John 5 and others, we can observe the process that produces the power to change. I want to identify ten simple things that you need to do to see a miracle of change in your life. I call them The Ten Commandments of Change, and they will work if you work them.

DESIRE

Desire To Change. When Jesus finds this man (as he has found us), he had already been in his paralytic condition for 38 years.

Have you ever felt like you've had the same problem forever? Have you ever felt so hopeless that you thought even Jesus wouldn't or couldn't fix it?

Often it's the thing that we have grown accustomed to or learned to tolerate in our lives that we need to change.

But we see in John 5:6, the first thing Jesus said to the man was surely one of the most provocative questions ever put to anyone:

"Do you want to get well?"

Talk about an ice-breaker! He doesn't ask him how he's doing. He doesn't tell him how much he understands what life must have been like for the last 38 years. He gets right to root issue. "How bad do you want this?"

To change anything, you have to, first, desire it more than you desire just about anything. That's when things will begin to change for you. Jesus even said in one of the most famous passages of Scripture, "whatsoever things you *DESIRE*, when you pray, believe you have received them, and they shall be granted you" (Mark 11:24).

A young man was walking down a dock one day and he noticed a man fishing who he had read about and followed for many years. The young man desired to be a great salesman and the older man had been one of the best in the world. When he approached him, he asked the man what he needed in order to be great.

The old man grabbed his admirer and stuck his head under the water. The young man kicked and pushed and did everything he could to get up until he couldn't hold his breath any longer. When the young man finally fought his way out of the water, gasping for air with a furious attitude, he declared, "Are you crazy? I couldn't breathe!"

The man responded, "Son, when you want to succeed as much as you wanted to breathe, that's when you will become a great salesman and a great success."

So you have to desire to change. You need to admit you have a need and desire it as much as your breath.

To get results, we have to follow these principles—these commandments of change—and the first one is that we must desire it. We must want change. And without doing the things that it takes to change, then there is no change—and people who don't change will not grow.

There are several reasons why we don't desire change.

1. Fear. Our fear of change is that we don't believe we can change. We're afraid it won't work, so we don't try. But remember, God has given you the spirit of power—the power to change.

2. We perceive the need for change as an admission of weakness. It is not weak. It takes strength to admit the truth.

3. We don't like to unsettle things in our life. Why? We are settling for mediocrity when we could have a miracle. Remember, your miracle is often waiting in troubled and unsettled waters. Don't make it wait any longer!

If you have ever decided to clean out your desk or your closet, for example, you start out thinking you will tidy it up a bit. Then as you get into it, you realize how much there is. It begins to look worse as you are working on it. But it's all about to change—if you don't give up. It's about to get better no matter how messy it looks!

EXCUSES

Stop Making Excuses. The man responds to Jesus after being asked if he wants to be made whole, "'Sir, I have no man when the water is troubled to put me into the pool, but while I am coming another steps down before me'" (John 5:7).

How many times have we used the excuse, "I have no one to help me, no one to love me, no one to give me what I need?"

The next thing we need to do to release the power of change is: *we must stop making excuses.*

We know from history and from common sense, that the one who makes excuses fails. How can he succeed? He can't. Because there is always an excuse why he doesn't do what it takes to change or to succeed.

We call this a "victim mentality". And before we dismiss this as applying to someone else, ask yourself whether you have made excuses for the way things are. Because if you want things to change, you can no longer excuse them. This only gives them the right to stick around and bother you a little bit longer—maybe a lot longer.

Jesus didn't ask him if he had any friends to put him in the water. Friends are great. Don't get me wrong, but the times that change our lives are not when we have the moral support of loved ones—it's when we make the decision to do what needs to be done and look to man no further.

"Jesus said, 'Will you be made whole?' And the impotent man answered Him and said, '*Sir, I have no man*.'

Jesus didn't say, "Oh, I'm sorry that you don't have anyone to help you in. I feel really bad for you. I'll tell you what, let's pray about this."

Instead, Jesus told him to "Get up." He did not give this man a reason to continue making excuses.

Proverbs 26:13 says, "The sluggard says, 'There is a lion in the street so I can't go out now and work.'" What street does the sluggard live on? Why is he concerned abut lions in the street? He can't go to work because he's worried about *running into lions*? The point here is that a sluggard—a lazy man—will make up excuses that are just as ridiculous as 'a lion in the street'."

The Bible is full of examples of people that made excuses. Do you remember the story in Luke 14 about the man who invited people to the wedding feast of his master?

He goes to the first man and says, "The master has invited you to the wedding feast." And this man says, "I just bought a piece of land and I have got to go look at it." This is a ridiculous excuse. Who buys a piece of land before he looks at it?

He goes to the second man and says, "The master has invited you to the wedding."

And this man says, "I've just bought five yoke of oxen and I've got to go try them out." Who would buy five yoke of oxen before trying them out? Who would do something so ridiculous? Oxen were used for farming. In other words, this man's livelihood was dependent upon the oxen that supposedly he had just bought and had to go try out. Well, if your life depended on oxen, wouldn't you make sure that you tried them out before you bought them?

He goes to the third man and says, "The master has invited you to the wedding feast."

And this man says, "I just got married and for that reason I cannot come." Why not just bring your wife along?

All of these excuses are ridiculous. If we're going to see a change in our lives for the better, we've got to get to the point where we no longer make excuses.

We live in a society of excuse-making people. "I'm sorry I was late. I just ran into traffic." Everybody runs into traffic. You are the traffic! You knew there was going to be traffic.

"Oh, I'm sorry. I woke up late." What about your alarm clock? To put it in simple terms, if you wish to change, you have to remove every excuse from your life.

The person who makes the fewest number of excuses will be the person who becomes the most successful in life. From there we can just follow the curve—at the bottom of the scale. Whoever makes the most excuses will be the most unsuccessful. Where you fit on the curve of success will follow precisely along the line of your level of excuse-making.

Once you stop making excuses, you'll start doing the things you need to do.

"Well I tried to exercise but, you know, with all my kids and all their activities and all my responsibilities at work…" As long as we hide behind our responsibilities we will not change. Just do something! Everyone can do something.

God told Moses, "Take what you have in your hand and lift it up." That's when the miracles began to happen. Stop waiting for someone else to give you a miracle. Miracles began to happen for Moses when he took that staff in his hand and lifted it up. So take what you have in your hand and do something with what you have.

You've got to eliminate the whole idea of making excuses from your life, from your vocabulary, and from ever being a part of what you do.

At work, if your superior says, "Look, I want to know why this wasn't done." Don't say, "Well, so-and-so who works with us didn't carry his end." If he wanted to know what so-and-so did, he would have asked so-and-so. He asked you. You may think blaming so-and-so makes you look good for the moment, but any sharp employer will see right through that. He'll recognize that you're just shifting the blame on somebody else to take the attention off of what you didn't do. Don't blame it on somebody else. You can't honestly say that somebody else is the reason why you didn't do what you were supposed to do.

The best response in this situation, if you have fallen short, is to admit it. You say, "I take full responsibility. I have no excuse."

Have you ever been pulled over by a police officer? Inevitably, what do most of us do? We make excuses.

"But Officer, I'm late for work..." "But Officer, I didn't see the speed limit sign." "But Officer, I didn't see you behind me..."

Instead, just say, "Officer, I have no excuse. You are right and I am wrong (if you truly are). I would warmly welcome a warning."

I've learned that people are much more receptive to a person who owns up to what they have done than they ever will be to somebody that always has an excuse or who gets defensive. If we refuse to look at what needs to change in our lives, we are in denial and only hurting ourselves.

I hope you realize that you can look at an area of your life that needs to change without feeling condemned about it. God forgives you. He knows your struggles! You don't have to be condemned when you look at what needs to change, because God already knows what to do about it, and is working with you right now to bring His will to pass in your life (Philippians 2:12). But you must stop making excuses.

"I have no man!" the lame man said. But he didn't need one. He had Jesus–the miracle man–standing right in front of him ready to help. And so do you.

ACTION

Take Immediate Action. In John 5:8 (NKJ) Jesus went on to tell this man, "Rise, take up your bed and walk!"

The third commandment of change is take action. Do it now! Notice here, Jesus demanded immediate action from this man. He didn't ask him to run a marathon; he didn't ask him to climb a mountain. He told him to "GET UP". First things need to be first. Take a step. Do something you haven't been able to do. That's when something supernatural will begin to happen. You do what you can do in the natural. Then God will add His "super" to your "natural," resulting in "supernatural" power.

Sometimes it's something as simple as forgiving someone, or giving a gift to someone, giving an offering to God, praising

God when you don't feel like it. Don't worry if the progress is slow. Forget about what you haven't been able to do up until now.

What's stopping you? If you are like most people, you may question whether you can truly change. You may not believe things could ever change.

When this man started making excuses—"I have no man"—the first thing Jesus said was, "Rise, take up your pallet and walk." Jesus started giving him direction.

The way to break out of failure in life and an inability to change in life is to take immediate action.

You've got to walk before you run. You've got to run before you fly. But you have to start somewhere and you have to start now. It won't happen all at once. But you will grow.

Jesus said, "Rise." That's the first step. Then He said, "Take up your bed." He was saying, "Get your stuff." But He didn't tell him to get his stuff and get his act together, until he took the first step.

Often, we won't do anything until we think we can do everything. But it doesn't work that way. Nothing does. Everything starts with one simple act of obedience.

Remember when they came to Jesus and said they were out of wine? What did He tell them to do? "Fill the water pots with water!" But that didn't make sense. They needed wine! They needed a miracle. But it started with them taking immediate action and doing whatever Jesus told them to do.

Maybe you need a financial change. The Bible says, "Tithe." You may say, "That won't fix it." But it is the first action step that you know to take. And when you do, God will show you the next step, and your miracle will be waiting there. So take action now!

Don't wait for more money to come in. Don't wait for the right circumstances. Create the right circumstances by the seeds you sow (Ecclesiastes 11:1-6).

PERCEPTION

You Must Change How You See Yourself. Sometimes we have conditioned ourselves through time that things will always be the same. We must break that mentality.

There was a man who felt he was falling out of love with his wife. He consulted a friend of his who was a marriage counselor and he got the following advice: "Do some things for her that you would do if you were still in love with her. Get her some flowers. Some candy, a necklace. Shower her with love and gifts to show her how much you have changed.

He took the counselors advice and called him back with the following dilemma:

"I did what you told me," the man told his friend. "I decided to really change. Usually when I am done with work, I go home, sweaty and dirty, through the back door, get something to drink and sit out the couch watching television until my wife calls me for dinner."

"Well, this day I decided to do things differently. Before I went home after work, I took a shower, put a clean shirt on, stopped at the florist, bought some candy, and picked out a necklace that I thought my wife would like. I also put on some cologne, which I hadn't done in years. Instead of going through the back door, I came to the front door and rang the doorbell."

"When my wife opened the door she started crying hysterically! I asked her what was wrong and she said, 'Today has been terrible. Billy broke his leg, the washing machine broke, your mother called and said she was coming over for 3 weeks; and if that's not bad enough, *you had to come home drunk!*'"

You see, often we have been conditioned by the past to believe that this is the way things will always be. We don't believe it when the opportunity for real change comes.

If we're going to see change in our lives, we must raise our expectations. We must believe! Jesus declared in Mark 9:23, "All things are possible to him that believes."

Stop replaying your mistakes. Stop replaying how you used to be. The past is over. Treat it like it's over.

Proverbs 23:7 says "As a man thinks within, so is he."

Phil Simms, a two-time Super Bowl champion quarterback, had thrown a game-losing interception against the San Francisco 49ers, several years ago. After losing the game, he dejectedly went to the sideline with his head hanging low. It was a critical moment in time. His coach, Bill Parcels, yelled to him, "Forget about it." This didn't faze the quarterback, so his coach grabbed him and yelled again in his face, "I said, forget about it!"

He had to get Simms to erase the picture he had in his mind of failure. And it worked.

The next time they played the 49ers in the playoffs, he played brilliantly; they won the game and went on to win the Super Bowl. What happened? He stopped replaying the past. He changed how he saw *himself*.

Jesus said, if we had the faith of a mustard seed, we could say to the mountain to be removed and it would obey us. Too often the mountain intimidates us. Or we "tough it out" and try to muster up enough faith to move the mountain. But Jesus said we only need a mustard seed of faith. A mustard seed is the smallest of all the seeds.

Why did Jesus say we only needed a mustard seed to move the great big mountain? Because Jesus expects us to see ourselves much bigger than the mountain. When we see ourselves bigger than the situation, bigger than our condition, then *a little faith* is all it will take to make that *little* mountain move!

In Genesis 1:26 God declares, "Let Us make man in Our Image after Our Likeness."

If God is bigger than the mountain, then so are you—because you are made in the image of God!

We read in John 5:9, "Immediately the man was made whole, and took up his bed and walked."

I believe that from the moment Jesus said, "Rise up," to the moment this man did in fact rise up, Jesus' words created a picture in the man's mind of a whole and healed body. "The Word of God is living and active," Hebrews 4:12 tells us.

It was that picture of himself that empowered him to receive his healing and stay healed.

Often, we may experience a miracle or breakthrough in our lives, but if we keep seeing ourselves the way we used to be, then we will eventually revert back to the way we were.

Often people feel like changing or they make some resolution, but because their inner image remains the same, so do they. Perhaps you've experienced a miracle at church or in prayer, but if your inner image remains the same, you will revert back to the picture you have of yourself.

We must paint a new picture of ourselves with the Word of God. Refuse to accept your old self-image. See yourself the way God sees you:

As a new creature (2 Corinthians 5:17).

As healed (I Peter 2:24).

As victorious (Romans 8:37).

As fearless (2 Timothy 1:7).

These are a few examples of how you should begin to see yourself; and as you do, things will begin to change in your life.

If you want to change your weight, you must see yourself differently. (I'm using this as an example of an area of change because it's something we all deal with on one level or another. Few of us are completely satisfied with our weight.)

You've got to stop walking around and saying, "I'm fat and I'll always be fat. I've got

fat genes, fat cells, fat blood, and fat parents."
You've got to stop seeing yourself that way,
and you've got to stop talking about yourself
that way. Don't measure yourself by a scale
or mirror. Measure yourself by the way God
sees you and what He says about you.

Stop seeing yourself as dumb. "Well I've
always been dumb. When somebody tells a
joke, I'm the last person to get it. I'm the last
person that graduated. I'm the last person
that passed that class and I had to go through

it three times." You have got to stop seeing yourself that way and stop talking about yourself that way.

Stop seeing yourself as a failure at home. "I'm not really a good parent. I've tried but I just don't know if I can raise my kids right."

Stop seeing yourself as poor. "I'm from a blue collar family and we've always had a blue collar income and we're always going to make blue collar money." The reason that you're always going to make blue collar money is because you see yourself as a blue collar person. "I'm always the one that has to be told what to do. I could never initiate things myself or figure out how to do things. I will never grow beyond what I've attained." Of course, there's nothing wrong with a blue collar job, but you've got to start seeing yourself as the owner of the company rather than just working for it.

If you wish to see change in your life, you need to start talking about your dreams and not your shortcomings. You need to see yourself in a new way. You need to talk about yourself in a new way. And things will begin to change.

NEVER GO BACK

Never Go Back. "Afterward Jesus found him in the temple and said unto him, 'Behold thou hast been made whole. Sin no more, lest the worse thing come unto thee'" (John 5:14).

The fifth commandment of change is to never go back. We have to break the old habits. We have to get out of the old ruts. If you want to see change in your life, you must never go back to the way things were.

Perhaps you had been hanging around the wrong crowd and then you got away from them. But one day, all of the sudden, you start to miss their coarse jesting and their dirty mouths and the laughing and the joking around that you used to do. It was filthy, but you miss it. You forget how filthy it was—you just remember the laughter. But if you do go back to those relationships, the Bible says you are "like a dog returning to its vomit" (Proverbs 26:11). You're like a sow returning to the mud and mire.

We have got to go forward and never go backward if we want to see change in our lives. We never go back to the old relationships. We never go back to the old way of thinking. We never go back to the old way of looking. We never go back to the old way of acting. We never go back to find the old things in our closet—we want to get rid of those old things.

If you say, "Okay, from this day forward I am not going to eat such and such anymore." Then don't eat it anymore. Don't say, "Oh, but I just can't help myself." Don't eat it. Don't go back.

I've seen people get into adultery and destroy their families because they have gotten close to somebody at work. They get entangled in an emotional relationship and begin committing emotional adultery—and emotional adultery is just as bad as physical adultery. Emotional adultery will lead to imaginations, which will lead to a hardening of your heart toward your spouse, which will lead to divorce. Divorce comes from a hardness of heart. Anything that brings a hardness of heart is going to contribute to adultery, so you need to stay away from unwise emotional entanglements.

I've had people come to me for counsel and say, "I need help in my marriage." "Okay, let's find out why" I say. "Are you in adultery?"

"No, I'm not in adultery."

"Are you in an affair?"

"No, I've never had an affair."

"Well, who do you hang out with at work?"

"Well, there is a girl that I do like to talk to every day," or "There is a man that really thinks highly of me and compliments me every day and tells me how good I look." And then I tell them, "Well look, if you really want to be free and you really want your marriage restored, you must stop hanging around this person. From this day forward, you never go back. You never go back and talk to them again. You never go back and fellowship with them again. You never go to lunch with them."

"Oh it's innocent," they say. "It's in the cafeteria. There are other people all around."

I don't care. You are still opening up your heart to them and it will hurt you. Don't go back. Don't ever go back.

John 5:14 says, "…And finding him in the temple, Jesus said you him, 'You have been made well, STOP SINNING, so nothing worse happens to you.'" In other words, your lifestyle didn't prevent your miracle, but if you don't live a new way, things are going to get worse. It's interesting to note here that Jesus is NOW confronting him about his sin. He never brought it up when He healed him, because God wants us to understand we cannot earn our healing through our holiness.

I think that believers often feel that they cannot receive anything from God until they get all the sin out of their life. And while I am not endorsing keeping the sin in your life, the two are often unrelated. Since Jesus told him to stop sinning AFTER He healed him, then we can know that sinlessness is not a pre-requisite to our healing.

Having said that, Jesus understands the law of seedtime and harvest. Whatever a man sows, he shall also reap. So although the man's faith and action brought about the miraculous power of God, in order to preserve his healing, he was going to have to change whatever he was doing that was opening the door to his previous, 38–year condition.

Furthermore, even though he was healed, Jesus wanted him to know that there was something worse than having sickness—it's having the consequences of bad decisions in our lives.

We see a significant change in this man's life who was healed by Jesus. After being healed, where do we find him? He is in the temple–he is in church. He is learning a new way of thinking and seeing himself. He is not hanging around the same crowd or the same pool. He is now in God's house. He is now identifying with a new life.

He realized that the place to be was in the house of God where he could hear the life-changing Word that would empower him to become a victor rather than a victim. God's been good to you, now change!

What does this look like, practically?

1. Plant different seeds than the ones you've been planting.

2. Develop new relationships with people who will support and reinforce your change.

3. Get in the temple and learn to walk with God.

4. Change the way you think and you will change the way you live.

STOP WAITING

Stop Waiting For Someone Else To Do It. "This commandment which I command you this day is not hidden from thee, neither is it far off. It is not in heaven, that you should say, 'Who will go up for us to heaven? And bring it unto us, that we may hear it and do it?' Neither is it beyond the sea that you should say, 'Who shall go over the sea for us and bring it to us that we may hear it and do it?' But the Word is near unto thee, in thy mouth and in thy heart, that thou mayest do it" (Deuteronomy 30:11-14).

The sixth commandment of change is to stop waiting for someone else to do something. Stop waiting for someone to change before you change. Stop waiting for somebody to help you change. This principle is particularly relevant to people that are married and are constantly using their marriage as an excuse as to why they haven't changed—"Well, as soon as my husband changes then I'm going to change" or "As soon as my wife changes I'll stop doing that."

People often say, "Who will help me?" or "Who can I get to motivate me?" But you can't wait for someone to do it for you. God is your source and He will help you. But you must take the first step. It begins with your words. Speak to the mountains in your life! Too often we talk *about* the mountain rather than *to* the mountain. Tell that thing that needs to change in your life...tell it what you want it to do. Then do something you've never done before.

Change is near you. It is in your mouth. The power you need is in your mouth. Proverbs 18:21 declares that "death and life are in the power of the tongue." Your words carry the power to change anything.

Words changed the world. Words changed the weather. Words will change your circumstances and your life, but as long as you are looking for someone to do something for you, you will minimize the power and effectiveness of your own words.

YIELD

Yield To The Holy Spirit. "The wisdom that is from above is first pure, then peaceable, gentle, and easy to be entreated, full of mercy and good fruits, without partiality, and without hypocrisy" (James 3:17).

The seventh commandment of change is to learn to yield to the Holy Spirit. This is the greatest wisdom that you can have in life.

"Easy to be entreated" means willing to yield. It means that you're not so stubborn that somebody has to hit you over the head with a pan to get you to realize what you are doing wrong!

What does it mean to yield? When you come up to an intersection and you see a yield sign, what does that mean? It means that the other people going perpendicular to you have the right of way. So you wait until they have gone before you and then proceed.

A yield sign is not like a yellow light, which tells us to proceed with caution. To yield means to wait for the person who has the right to go before you, and then you follow after them.

This is what it means to yield to the Holy Spirit. We stop and allow the Holy Spirit to get in front of us, and then we follow Him and do what He tells us to do. We don't want to get ahead of the Holy Spirit.

Learn to yield to His voice. Don't wait for a bolt of lightning or listen for His voice in a clap of thunder. Don't look for a magical, mystical revelation. The Holy Spirit lives inside you.

Think about that a moment—how loud can a voice inside you be? It can only be as loud as anything else you hear in your inner ear. The Holy Spirit lives on the inside of you and you need to learn to yield to Him.

How do you know when you are yielding to the Holy Spirit?

The Holy Spirit will never tell you to do something contrary to the Word of God. He will never tell you to do something contrary to sound principles from the Word of God.

For example, how could someone say the Holy Spirit was telling him to get a different wife? That clearly contradicts the Bible.

Someone may ask, "Well, isn't there a place for divorce in the Bible? Isn't there a place in Scripture for remarriage?" Not when I'm already married. Not when I have the Bible and the Holy Spirit inside me and a willing marriage partner that is willing to live by the Word of God—even if the two people in this marriage don't see everything eye to eye.

We don't need to see everything eye to eye. We need to see everything according to what God's Word says.

What would happen if both people in a marriage said, "You know what? My opinion doesn't matter. Your opinion doesn't matter.

Let's find out what the Word of God says about this." That's a marriage that's going to make it.

God is not as mysterious as some people think. He reveals Himself to us through the Bible.

But the Holy Spirit needs yielded vessels. He will speak to you. You can hear His voice. But when you do, yield! I can't tell you how many people I've watched over the years whose stubborness prevented them from changing. It's easy to get set in our ways.

We can grow accustomed to the way things are. We can get used to misery. We learn how to cope with it. But God didn't call us to cope with misery (Psalm 32:9). Yield to Him. Follow His leading. Trust His Word and things will change!

DREAM

Never Stop Dreaming. "'It shall come to pass in the last days,' saith God, 'I will pour out my Spirit upon all flesh; and your sons and your daughters shall prophesy, and your young men shall see visions, and your old men shall dream dreams'" (Acts 2:17).

The eighth commandment of change is you must never stop dreaming.

If you want to see change in your life, you've got to dream about the things that God says you can dream about.

Sometimes we think dreaming is just for kids and the young people that have their future in front of them. But the Bible says, "Your old men shall dream dreams." I believe a man is not old until regrets take the place of dreams. Never stop dreaming. You may say, "I'm 50 years old." "I'm 60 years old." "I'm 70 years old." "I'm stuck right where I am." But that's not true. Never stop dreaming. You could write a book that could be a best seller. You could make a record that could go platinum. You could do something great. You could create something great. You could come up with an idea. You could come up with an invention. You could reinvent yourself. Are you willing to reinvent yourself?

Are you willing to change to the degree that you say, "I want to see change in my life. I don't like the way things are. I don't like the status quo. I don't like the mediocre and the average. I am ready to reinvent myself. I am ready for God to change me."

Psalm 126:1 says, "When the Lord turned back the captive ones of Zion, we were like those who dream."

We should never stop dreaming. I don't mean daydreaming. "We were like those who dream" means a dream with some action points to follow it.

In my own life there are many things that the Lord has called me to do. There are some dreams that He's put in my heart and some visions that He's put in my heart.

I could have a tendency to get comfortable with my life, but it is His dreams that keep me going, changing, adapting, so I can see better days. After building a successful church, God put a dream in my heart to reach the inner city. So we started a church there. After doing that, God put a dream in my heart to build a new ministry campus four times the size of the first one.

He put a dream in my heart to reach the world through television. What started as a little basement video is now reaching upwards of potentially half a billion people! But I keep going because of those dreams.

Joseph endured much and was able to pass many tests because he kept dreaming.

People will malign you. Some will not believe you. Others may try to hurt you. But God will protect the dreamer and the dream.

Unfortunately many people are just talkers. There are too many people out there talking about the things they want to do, and talking about the dreams they have, but they never put wheels to it. We've got to take our dream and we've got to put some action behind it and put a plan with it.

In my life, the Lord has already shown me what I am to believe for within the next three years, and what I am to believe for within five years. He has awakened in me a ten-year dream and a twenty-year dream as well.

I have enough money to be happy. I'm successful enough to be happy. But that's not what keeps me going. I don't want to settle for less than His dreams for my life. What makes me happy is fulfilling the purpose for which God has created me. Dreaming big dreams makes me happy. I don't want to ever stop dreaming and putting plans to those dreams.

What about you? You can start a new business if you want to. It doesn't take a lot. It just takes a product and a plan. It just takes an idea. You could start a restaurant. You could start a hot dog stand. You could start anything. You could succeed at anything. You must dream it. You must see it. If you can see it, you can have it. If you can see it, it can happen. I don't mean you see it with your natural eye, I mean you see it on the inside.

You can do anything and succeed at it if you're willing to dream and if you're willing to take a risk and if you're willing to create a plan. But then you must be willing to work that plan and be devoted to that plan and be committed to that plan.

You know you are the righteousness of God, don't you? You know you're going to Heaven. You know God's on your side. So do something with it!

It won't always be easy. 2 Corinthians 4:17 says, "For our light affliction, which is but for a moment, worketh for us a far more exceeding and eternal weight of glory."

If you're going to change, that change may bring some light affliction. Change may bring some momentary affliction. Change doesn't always feel good. Sometimes change hurts. But it's only a light affliction, and it's working in you "a far more exceeding and eternal weight of glory."

We see how this works in the next verse: "While we look not at the things that are seen, but at the things that are not seen; for the things which are seen are temporary, but the things which are not seen are eternal" (2 Corinthians 4:18).

We're looking at something—but we're not looking at things that we see with our physical eyes. We're looking at the unseen things. The things that we see are temporary and subject to change, but the things which are not seen are eternal.

So, if you want to see something change in your life, you've got to see it on the inside.

What's inside you is eternal and what's around you is temporal–it is subject to change. The eternal is always greater than the temporary.

Let's say there is a physical sickness in your body that needs to change. What is greater than that physical sickness that you see in your body?

The Word of God.

The reason why the Word is greater than sickness is because sickness is temporary and the Word is eternal. Only an eternal thing can change a temporary thing. Temporary things do not have authority over temporary things. But eternal things have authority over temporary things.

You could get saved and never apply any of the other teaching of the Bible, but when you die and go to Heaven, you will be healed. Why? Because healing is eternal. And sickness is temporary. In eternity the eternal things will rule over the temporary things—completely, and without challenge.

But in this life the eternal things—which are the promises of God's Word—are challenged by the temporary things that we see with our eyes.

So, we have to overcome the challenges of what we see by applying what we don't see (the promises of God) to the things we do see. Speak God's Word, think God's Word, do God's Word! This is a part of dreaming His dreams, and it will cause things to change!

PURPOSE

Know Why You Are Here. "For whom He did foreknow, He predestinated to be conformed to the image of His Son that He might be the firstborn among many brethren" (Romans 8:29).

The ninth commandment of change is you must have purpose. One of the reasons that people don't change is because they really don't know why they are here on this earth. They don't know their purpose in life. When you know your purpose, you are going to change.

People who stay the same are people who don't have a goal greater than where they are right now. I don't believe our goals should be limited to monetary goals or career-minded goals. I believe we should narrow down our goals to God's purpose for our lives, and then we should be willing to do whatever it takes to obtain that purpose at any cost. If you don't have a greater goal than where you're at right now, it's because you don't know God's goal for your life. Write down, now, what you believe God wants you to do and what you're believing for. Then it will be easy to admit your need to change and to identify the costs and risks you need to take to see that change.

The Bible says the purpose for which you are on this planet is to be conformed to the image of the Son of God. You are here to be changed into His image. On the inside, you already do look like Jesus. Your spirit already looks like Him. But your mind and your attitudes don't look quite like Him yet—so they must be conformed to the image of Jesus.

So if this is to be your goal in life, how do you achieve it? By renewing your mind.

If you are going to be conformed in the image of Jesus, you need to renew your mind through the Word of God. You need to re-educate your mind to think in line with God's Word.

Why don't more Jews get saved? Why don't more Muslims get saved? I suspect it's because Christians are such a bad example of who Jesus really is.

When people see the real Jesus, they will get saved. If our lives would reflect who Jesus really is, then Jews would get saved and Muslims would get saved and our cousins would get saved and our uncles would get saved and our aunts would get saved and all our other relatives would get saved. All these people will start getting saved as we become conformed to the image of Jesus! This is your purpose. Let nothing distract you.

DON'T BE AFRAID

Don't Be Afraid of Losing What You Have. "'If you really want to follow Me,' Jesus said to the rich young ruler, 'then sell what you have, give away to the poor and come follow me. You will have treasure in Heaven'" (see Matthew 19:21).

The tenth commandment of change is to not be afraid of losing what you have.

If what you have is from God, then there is no need to be afraid of losing it. If it's from God, and you do lose it, then God can get it back to you. If it's not from God, then why are you afraid of losing it? If something is not from God, then you should want to get it out of your life.

So don't be afraid of losing what you have.

Tragically, the rich young ruler was unwilling to lose what he had. And because he was unwilling to let it go, he was never able to embrace what God had for him.

So what about you?

Is there anything for which you are holding on too tightly? Sometimes our hands are so full of what we think is valuable, that we cannot receive what is truly valuable—what God wants to give us.

Jesus said, "He who finds his life shall lose it, but he who loses his life or My sake shall find it" (Mark 8:35).

Let me leave you with this thought: whatever you give to God, will come back to you better than before.

- Abraham gave Isaac and he got the nations of the world.

- The widow gave her last meal and she received a year of supply.

- The woman gave her ointment, and she received Jesus' protection and blessing.

Whenever we think we are giving something up, we must remember God knows what He's doing and always has something better for us.

THE TEN COMMANDMENTS OF CHANGE

1. Desire To Change. "And a certain man was there which had an infirmity thirty-eight years and when Jesus saw him lying there He knew that he had been a long time in that case and He said, **'Will you be made whole?'**" (John 5:5-6).

2. *Stop Making Excuses.* "Jesus said, 'Will you be made whole?' And the impotent man answered Him and said, '***Sir, I have no man*** when the water is troubled to put me into the pool, but while I am coming another steps down before me'" (John 5:6-7).

3. *Take Immediate Action.* "Jesus said unto him, 'Rise, take up your bed and walk'" (John 5:8).

4. Change How You See Yourself.
"Immediately the man was made whole, and took up his bed and walked" (John 5:9).

5. Never Go Back. "Afterward Jesus found him in the temple and said unto him, 'Behold thou hast been made whole. Sin no more, lest the worse thing come unto thee'" (John 5:14).

6. Stop Waiting For Someone Else To Do It. "This commandment which I command you this day is not hidden from thee, neither is it far off. It is not in heaven, that you should say, 'Who will go up for us to heaven? And bring it unto us, that we may hear it and do it?' Neither is it beyond the sea that you should say, 'Who shall go over the sea for us and bring it to us that we may hear it and do it?' But the word is near unto thee, in thy mouth and in thy heart, that thou mayest do it" (Deuteronomy 30:11-14).

7. *Yield to the Holy Spirit.* "The wisdom that is from above is first pure, then peaceable, gentle, and easy to be entreated, full of mercy and good fruits, without partiality, and without hypocrisy" (James 3:17).

8. Never Stop Dreaming. "'It shall come to pass in the last days,' saith God, 'I will pour out my Spirit upon all flesh; and your sons and your daughters shall prophesy, and your young men shall see visions, and your old men shall dream dreams'" (Acts 2:17).

9. Know Why You Are Here. "For whom He did foreknow, He predestinated to be conformed to the image of His son that He might be the firstborn among many brethren" (Romans 8:29).

10. Don't Be Afraid of Losing What You Have. "'If you really want to follow me,' Jesus said to the rich young ruler, 'then sell what you have, give away to the poor and come follow me. You will have treasure in Heaven'" (see Matthew 19:21).

Concluding Thoughts

Remember it's never too late. The man at the pool of Bethesda was in that condition for 38 years. It doesn't matter how long you've been the way you are. It doesn't matter how long that situation has been in your life. Now you have the power to change that circumstance! You don't need a man—you have The Man—Jesus Christ, standing right in front of you asking, "Do you want to be made whole?"

If your answer is "yes," take the first step, follow these commandments of change and get ready for God to do exceedingly abundantly beyond what you can ask or think!

ABOUT THE AUTHOR

Gregory Dickow is the host of "Changing Your Life," a dynamic television show seen throughout the world, reaching a potential 450 million households. He is also the founder and Senior Pastor of Life Changers International Church, a diverse and thriving congregation in the Chicago area with several thousand in weekly attendance.

Known for his ability to communicate the power and principles of God's Word clearly and concisely, Pastor Dickow lives to see the lives of people dramatically changed forever.

Pastor Dickow is also founder of Valeo International, a family of churches and ministries committed to spreading the Gospel of Jesus Christ, planting churches, and making disciples around the world.

Other Books Available by Pastor Gregory Dickow

- Acquiring Beauty
- Breaking the Power of Inferiority
- Conquering Your Flesh
- Financial Freedom
- How to Hear the Voice of God
- How to Never Be Hurt Again
- Taking Charge of Your Emotions
- The Power to Change Anything
- Winning the Battle of the Mind

Audio Series available by Pastor Gregory Dickow

- Financial Freedom: Strategies for a Blessed Life
- How to Pray & Get Results
- Love Thyself
- Mastering Your Emotions
- Redeemed from the Curse
- The Blood Covenant
- Building Your Marriage God's Way

You can order these and many other life-changing materials by calling toll-free 1-888-438-5433.

For more information about Gregory Dickow Ministries and a free product catalog, please visit *www.changinglives.org*